# WACKY WORLD of SPORTS

# WACKY IN THE WATER

## Alix Wood

Gareth Stevens
PUBLISHING

Please visit our website, **www.garethstevens.com**. For a free color catalog of all our high-quality books, call toll free 1-800-542-2595 or fax 1-877-542-2596.

Library of Congress Cataloging-in-Publication Data

Wood, Alix.
Wacky in the water / by Alix Wood.
p. cm. — (Wacky world of sports)
Includes index.
ISBN 978-1-4824-1267-3 (pbk.)
ISBN 978-1-4824-1240-6 (6-pack)
ISBN 978-1-4824-1496-7 (library binding)
1. Aquatic sports — Juvenile literature. 2. Extreme sports — Juvenile literature. I. Wood, Alix. II. Title.
GV770.5 W66 2015
797—d23

First Edition

Published in 2015 by
**Gareth Stevens Publishing**
111 East 14th Street, Suite 349
New York, NY 10003

© Alix Wood Books

Produced for Gareth Stevens by Alix Wood Books
Designed by Alix Wood
Picture and content research: Kevin Wood
Editor: Eloise Macgregor

Photo credits:
Cover, 1, 4, 5 bottom, 7 bottom, 8-9, 10, 11 top, 12, 13, 16, 17, 19 top, 26 top, 28-29 © Shutterstock; 5 top, 6 top © iStock; 6, 18, 24-25 © Corbis; 11 middle © Peter Nawrocky; 11 bottom © Arjes; 14-15 © Juliet Eden/Dreamstime; 19 bottom © Dreamstime; 20 inset © Cmglee; 20-21 © Sgt. Michael Baltz/DoD; 24 inset © Verne Equinox; 26 © Velela; 27 top © David Underwater; 27 bottom © Hu Totya.

Printed in the United States of America

CPSIA compliance information: Batch # CS15GS: For further information contact Gareth Stevens, New York, New York at 1-800-542-2595.

# Contents

Wacky sports can be dangerous. Do not attempt any of the sports in this book without supervision from a trained adult expert!

# Wacky Water Sports

There are lots of crazy sports that people do on or in the water. Snorkeling in a muddy bog, playing hockey underwater, performing dangerous tricks on a Jet Ski, or rowing in a hollowed-out pumpkin are just a few examples. Swimming in freezing cold water has to be one of the oddest ways to "chill out!" Many people in Finland go ice swimming after a hot sauna. They often place a heated carpet leading from the sauna to the hole in the ice. This prevents the drips from the swimmers from forming a dangerous, icy path!

## WACKY FACT

Ice swimming is very popular in Finland. Ninety percent of the population has tried ice swimming, and around 120,000 people in the country do it regularly!

Ice swimmers recommend **exhaling** as you jump in. This helps your lungs and rib cage cope with the shock as the cold water hits you.

# WACKY SPORTS NEWS

There is an International Ice Swimming organization. In order to become a member, people have to:

- have completed a swim of at least one mile (1.6 km);
- have no help while they swim;
- wear a swimming costume or briefs, swimming cap, and goggles while swimming. They must not wear a wetsuit, and;
- swim in water temperatures at or below 41°F (5°C).

Winter swimming can be dangerous. The sudden cold temperature can cause heart problems and **shock**. It is important never to swim alone. Swimmers need to gradually teach their bodies to get used to the sudden cold by doing regular short swims. Ice swimming can be good for you too, though. Winter swimmers are said to suffer less stress, have a better memory, feel better, and be more active.

The bodies of children and the elderly cool down too quickly to be able to go ice swimming.

# Bog Snorkeling

Bog snorkelers must swim two lengths of a murky trench cut out of a peat bog using only flippers to **propel** themselves! The Bog Snorkeling Championships take place every year in a peat bog near Llanwrtyd Wells, Wales. Both Ireland and Australia hold their own national championships, too. Some athletes take the championships very seriously. Some don't!

Llanwrtyd Wells, Wales

A competitor at the start of the Northern Ireland Bog Snorkeling Championships.

START

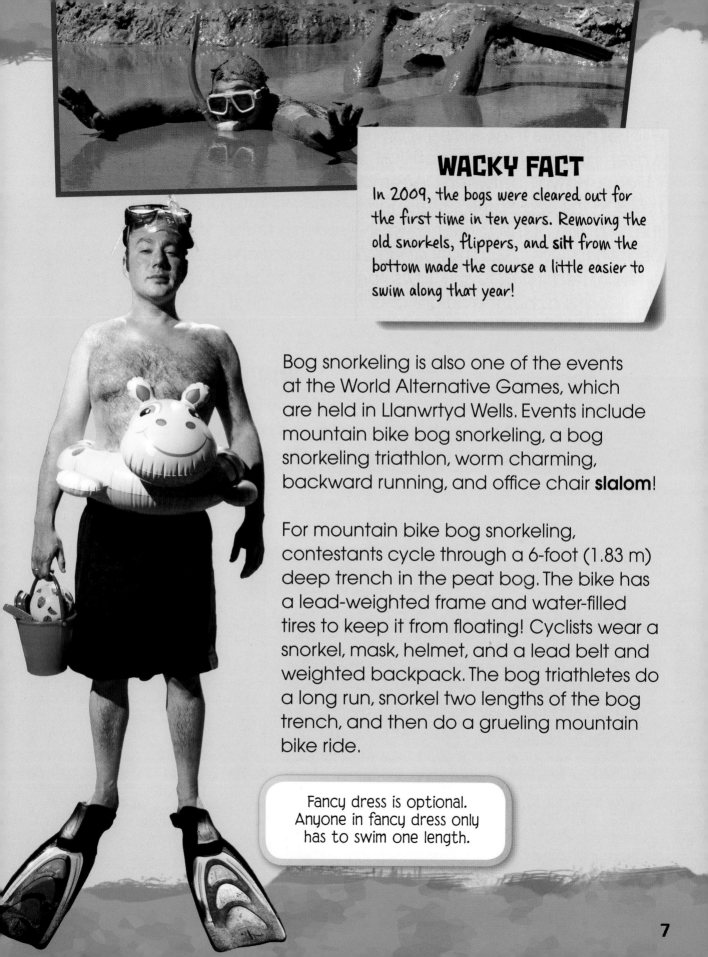

In 2009, the bogs were cleared out for the first time in ten years. Removing the old snorkels, flippers, and **silt** from the bottom made the course a little easier to swim along that year!

Bog snorkeling is also one of the events at the World Alternative Games, which are held in Llanwrtyd Wells. Events include mountain bike bog snorkeling, a bog snorkeling triathlon, worm charming, backward running, and office chair **slalom**!

For mountain bike bog snorkeling, contestants cycle through a 6-foot (1.83 m) deep trench in the peat bog. The bike has a lead-weighted frame and water-filled tires to keep it from floating! Cyclists wear a snorkel, mask, helmet, and a lead belt and weighted backpack. The bog triathletes do a long run, snorkel two lengths of the bog trench, and then do a grueling mountain bike ride.

Fancy dress is optional. Anyone in fancy dress only has to swim one length.

# Surfing Jaws

A lot of people think surfing is a pretty ordinary activity. Surfing the waves they call "Jaws" is not! Just off the north coast of the island of Maui, Hawaii, between December and March, enormous waves break in the sea. Some surfers named the large waves "Jaws" after the 1975 film of the same name. The surfers thought the waves' deadliness was like a shark attack. Even experienced surfers have been injured trying to surf Jaws. The waves can be 70 feet (21.3 m) high! That's about the height of a 7-story building!

## WACKY FACT

Usually surfers can't just paddle into Jaws like they can a normal wave. The waves move too fast. Surfers have to get towed to the wave by a Jet Ski or speedboat.

## WACKY SPORTS NEWS

A Jaws surfing contest is held in Maui. The best big wave surfers are invited to compete. Surfers have to wait for the right conditions before the competition can start. This can mean a lot of waiting around, sometimes for months! The waves have to be between 30 and 50 feet (9.1 and 15.2 m) high, with the right type of wind from the right direction. The special conditions are necessary because for this competition, the surfers must paddle into the waves rather than use Jet Skis.

Maui, Hawaii

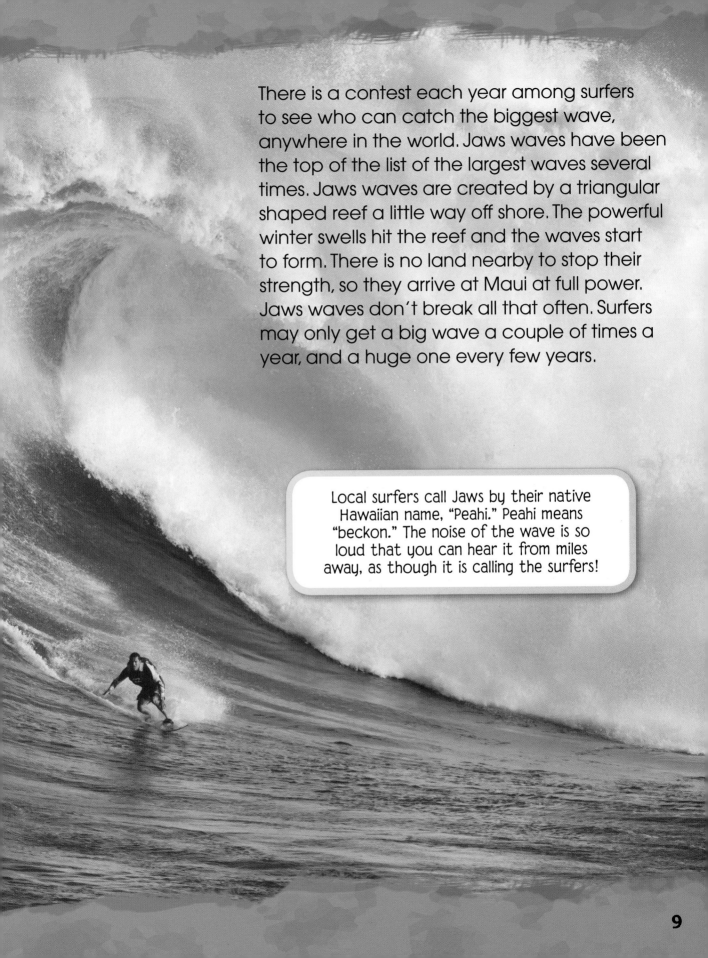

There is a contest each year among surfers to see who can catch the biggest wave, anywhere in the world. Jaws waves have been the top of the list of the largest waves several times. Jaws waves are created by a triangular shaped reef a little way off shore. The powerful winter swells hit the reef and the waves start to form. There is no land nearby to stop their strength, so they arrive at Maui at full power. Jaws waves don't break all that often. Surfers may only get a big wave a couple of times a year, and a huge one every few years.

Local surfers call Jaws by their native Hawaiian name, "Peahi." Peahi means "beckon." The noise of the wave is so loud that you can hear it from miles away, as though it is calling the surfers!

# Cave Diving

Cave diving is a crazy and dangerous sport. Once a diver has entered an underwater cave, finding the surface again in an emergency isn't easy. If divers have traveled a long way into the cave, it can be difficult for them to retrace their steps. It is hard to see. Divers will be in complete darkness if their flashlight fails, and the water is often very murky. Caves can have strong natural currents to deal with, too.

Divers dive together for safety, but they can rarely help one another if they get into trouble. Each diver needs to be responsible for their own safety.

The best area for underwater caves is the Yucatán Peninsula in Mexico. This region has over 100 different cave entrances and miles of beautiful passageways.

Cave diving in Mexico.

This diver is wearing his tank on his side to help fit through the narrow gap in the cave.

# WACKY FACT

Cave divers try not to kick the bottom, as it stirs up the dirt and makes the water murky. Cave divers use a technique called "pull and glide." Using their fingers (left), divers hold onto holes in the rock and pull themselves along, gliding through the cave.

# WACKY SPORTS NEWS

To find their way back to the surface, cave divers tie a guideline to a point at the cave entrance. They usually tie the guideline around two separate objects to make sure it doesn't come untied. The guideline marks the direction of the exit with arrows. Here, a cave diver is tying his own line to the main guideline so he can explore a cave off to the right in safety.

new guideline

main guideline with arrows

# Hydroflying

Hydroflying is a new way of getting around on the water! The rider stands on a board that's connected by a long hose to a **personal watercraft**, such as a Jet Ski. The hose pumps water to a pair of jet boots and also sometimes to a pair of handheld stabilizers. The rider controls the board by moving his feet and moving the jets on the stabilizers.

## WACKY FACT

Hydroflying is a very new sport. The board was only invented in 2011.

The person on the hydroboard can steer themselves, but the **throttle** is controlled by a person on the Jet Ski.

To start hydroflying, the rider lies facedown in the water and bends his knees. When the water starts flowing though the hose, it forces the rider straight up into the air! Riders can dive into the water, too. They can get pushed along underwater and jump out again like a dolphin!

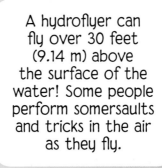

A hydroflyer can fly over 30 feet (9.14 m) above the surface of the water! Some people perform somersaults and tricks in the air as they fly.

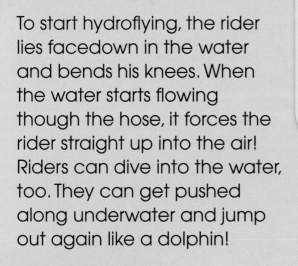

boots

board

# WACKY SPORTS NEWS

Hydroflying needs a lot of equipment. A Jet Ski, board, and boots are the bare minimum. The rider straps his feet into the boots. The boots are strapped onto the board using bindings like those on a wakeboard. Water flows to the board through a long, wide fire hose. A helmet and wetsuit are pretty essential, too.

# christmas Day swim

Swimmers dress up in fancy dress and take to the water on one of the coldest days of the year! Christmas Day swims are traditional in many parts of the world, particularly the UK. Occasionally the sea is too rough. In Brighton, England, the red warning flags were put on the beach in 2012 and the swim had to be abandoned. The Brighton Swimming Club members had taken a Christmas Day dip every year since 1860!

## WACKY SPORTS NEWS

The Serpentine is a lake in Hyde Park, London, England. Since 1864, the Serpentine Swimming Club has held a 100-yard (91.4 m) swimming competition every Christmas morning. In 1904, the author J. M. Barrie awarded the Peter Pan Cup to the winner of the race. The cup has been presented every year since. The race is open only to members of the club.

London, England

In Porthcawl, Wales, around 900 swimmers have been known to get into the sea on Christmas Day! Many arrive in fancy dress. Around 2,000 people come to the beach to watch, too. Swimmers of all ages take the walk to the beach from the local restaurant, the Hi-Tide Inn. Collections are made for local charities.

Porthcawl, Wales

The Christmas Day swim at Porthcawl, Wales.

# Jet Ski Freestyle

Jet Ski freestyle is amazing to watch. Jet Ski riders do tricks on their personal watercraft. The Jet Skis are propelled by water jets. Riders can sit, stand, or kneel on the Jet Skis. It's a little like doing motocross stunts in the water. Tricks include backflips, barrel rolls, tail stands, and even riding under the water!

Some freestylers do a trick called a "submarine." This involves jumping the Jet Ski in the air and then plunging underwater. The rider and Jet Ski pop back out of the water a distance away from where he went under!

No-handed routines take a lot of balance and courage.

## WACKY FACT

In 2008, a 14-year-old, Jack Moule, won the UK national championship! On a TV program three years later, he was challenged to complete five barrel rolls and one backflip in 60 seconds. He managed to do it in 52 seconds!

# WACKY SPORTS NEWS

The International Jet Ski World Finals takes place every year in Lake Havasu City, Arizona. Jet Skiers have to be invited to compete. Competitors come from all around the world to take part. They have a slalom race where competitors zigzag around markers and a race around a circuit with left and right turns. At the freestyle event, the competitors have two minutes to impress the judges with their maneuvers!

Lake Havasu City, Arizona

A Jet Skier doing a backflip.

# Log Rolling

Log rolling involves two people standing on a floating log. The log rollers spin the log in the water backward and forward with their feet. This competition is called a "roleo." Rollers try to stop or turn the log suddenly to get their opponent off-balance and into the water. Each match is timed. If no one falls off the log in the set time, the opponents move on to a smaller log.
Smaller logs don't float as well and are harder to roll. Log rollers usually wear spiked shoes to help them grip on the log. They also carry a long pike to steady themselves, which they throw to one side when the match starts.

A log roller overbalances.

# WACKY SPORTS NEWS

The sport of log rolling came from the days when **lumberjacks** used to bring their logs downriver to the sawmills. To help keep the logs rolling, lumberjacks would stand on them and roll them down the river! Logjams like the one pictured left would happen if they didn't keep the logs moving. Lumberjacks held competitions in their free time to see who could stay on the logs the longest.

## WACKY FACT

The main trick to being a good log roller is to never take your eyes off your opponent's feet. That way, you can see what they are about to do and be ready.

A log roller's knees must always be bent. The lower you are, the more balanced you are. Rollers must always keep their feet moving and use small, quick steps.

Log rolling on a makeshift lake at a competition.

# Cardboard Raft Races

What would be one of the worst materials to make a raft from? Cardboard, perhaps? Cardboard raft races are very wacky. Competitors are normally given a set time to make their raft. They can usually only use cardboard, tape, and glue. The paddles have to be made from cardboard, too. The rafts are then raced. Most rafts flood and sink! The winning team is usually chosen for their creativity, as very rarely do any make it past the winning post!

## WACKY FACT

The earliest known cardboard boat race was held at Southern Illinois University in 1962. A tutor at the university gave his design students the task of designing a cardboard boat that would carry a person for 100 feet (30.48 m). Points were awarded for staying dry, making the fastest time, and spending the least on the materials.

To celebrate the end of their exams, university students from Cambridge University, England, hold a cardboard boat race.

# WACKY SPORTS NEWS

One of the largest cardboard boat races takes place in Heber Springs, Arkansas. The boats have to be built completely out of cardboard. They can be given a coat of varnish or clear paint. The boats can only be held together at the seams with duct tape. Three or four boats compete against each other at once, and usually as many as 50 boats compete altogether!

Heber Springs, Arkansas

US Air Force airmen paddle their cardboard boat in the annual Cardboard Boat Regatta at Hurlburt Field, Florida.

# Kite Boarding

Kite boarding is fast and fun. It is a mixture of surfing, kite flying, and wakeboarding. The surfer uses the kite to catch the wind and drag themselves along the water. Kite boards are a lot like wakeboards, with straps on the top to hold the surfer's feet onto the board. The kite is the type used in paragliding, with a control bar to steer it with. If the wind is strong, kite boarders can reach speeds of 40 miles (64 km) per hour! The kite can allow the kite boarder to jump more than 30 feet (10 m) in the air. It's an exciting sport!

control bar

harness

foot strap

A kite boarder getting pulled along a wave.

A kite boarder showing why you need straps on your board!

Kite boarding can be dangerous. The lines can be up to 100 feet (30 m) long and can get tangled and cause accidents. High winds can blow you far offshore. Kite boarders have been injured crashing into buildings or trees, being attacked by sharks, or being electrocuted by overhead power lines! Hitting the water at speed is called having a "kitemare!" It can hurt! Kites have also been known to hurt **bystanders** on the beach when they crash down to earth.

## WACKY SPORTS NEWS

You don't just have to kite board on the sea. You can kite board on lakes. Some people kite board on ice, dirt, sand, grass, or snow, too! The equipment that you need can pack up small enough to fit in a backpack. The board is usually light and can be carried easily under one arm.

# Pumpkin Regattas

Competitions to grow the largest pumpkin have taken place for many years. But what should you do with all the enormous pumpkins after that? Hollow them out and race them up and down the river, according to the people of Windsor, Nova Scotia. Pumpkin racing began there in 1999. Today, races are held in several other towns around the US and Canada. It is certainly wacky to watch!

**WACKY FACT**

In Damariscotta, Maine, they hold a 10-day Pumpkinfest! With pumpkin-eating contests and pumpkin art, the pumpkin regatta is the final exciting event.

The pumpkins are very heavy. They have to be moved to the water using a forklift truck!

Paddlers race their giant pumpkins across Lake Pesaquid, Windsor.

Pumpkin races usually include a rowing race and a motorized race. Powerboat pumpkins can travel at quite a speed once they are fitted with a 15 horsepower engine! Many pumpkins have been known to sink, however, as they often tip over!

# Underwater Hockey

Hockey is a pretty ordinary sport, but not if you play it underwater! Sometimes called "octopush," it is played all over the world by teams armed with a snorkel and a tiny hockey stick. Two teams compete to hit a small **puck** along the bottom of the pool toward the opposition's goals. They have no breathing equipment apart from a snorkel, so if they need air, they have to swim to the surface.

Six players on each team are in the water at any one time, with another four players waiting on the poolside to be **substitutes**. They play two halves of either ten or fifteen minutes each, with a small break between them. Teams switch ends at halftime.

A team racing to the center of the pool at the start of a game of underwater hockey.

## WACKY FACT

To start a game, the puck is put on the bottom at the center of the pool. The players wait by the poolside for a signal. Then both teams swim fast above water to the middle of the pool toward the puck.

It's important to be able to hold your breath for a long time and be a great swimmer.

The rules are much like those for normal hockey. Penalties are given to players for hitting each other with sticks and getting their bodies in the way of the puck or a player with the puck. For a penalty, players can be taken out of the game, the other team can be given possession, or they can be given a penalty shot.

## WACKY SPORTS NEWS

Players wear a mask to help them see and to protect their faces. The masks have two lenses to make them strong in case they are hit with the puck. Fins help players swim faster through the water. One team plays with black sticks and the other with white. Players wear a glove to stop their hand from getting sore rubbing on the bottom of the pool. The puck is made of lead and covered in plastic. The referees wear orange gloves, a golden shirt, and red hat and communicate using hand signals.

# Waterfall Kayaking

**Whitewater** kayaking is pretty dangerous. Kayaking down an enormous waterfall takes it to another level of crazy. Kayakers use either of two techniques, "boofing" or "penciling." Whichever one they choose depends on how tall the waterfall is. Boofing is holding your kayak out **at right angles** to the fall of the water so you land flat. Penciling is holding the kayak **vertically** and riding the water. The higher the waterfall, the more vertical you'll want to enter the water. If you boof, you hit the bottom flat and the force can hurt your back.

The Pelouse Falls in Washington.

## WACKY FACT

Waterfall kayaker Tyler Bradt has kayaked over the Pelouse Falls in Washington. The drop is 180 feet (54.9 m). That's the height of an 18-story building! If a kayaker lands badly or gets pinned under by the water, there is nothing anyone can do to help them. It is very dangerous.

# WACKY SPORTS NEWS

It seems a little weird to talk about safety precautions when you are about to kayak over the edge of a waterfall. There are some things that kayakers can do to make the experience safer, however! They can pad the seat and footrests to soften their landing. They can make sure their personal flotation device and their helmet are in good condition and fastened on tight. They can double-check that their boat is safe. They should also get an experienced safety team ready at the bottom of the waterfall.

The kayaks have blunt ends. These are less likely to get stuck in rocks than a pointed-ended kayak would be.

# Glossary

**at right angles**
Sticking out at 90 degrees.

**bystanders**
People standing near but taking no part in an event.

**exhaling**
Breathing out.

**lumberjacks**
Loggers.

**personal watercraft**
A recreational watercraft such as a Jet Ski.

**propel**
To push or drive usually forward or onward.

**puck**
A disk used in hockey.

**shock**
A state of bodily collapse often marked by a drop in blood pressure, usually caused by a severe injury.

**silt**
A deposit of sediment.

**slalom**
Moving in a zigzag or wavy course between upright poles.

**substitutes**
People who take the place of another, especially in sport.

**throttle**
A valve controlling the flow of steam or fuel to an engine.

**vertically**
Straight up or down from a level surface.

**whitewater**
A river or creek that has a lot of rapids that create frothing white water.

# For More Information

**Books**

Evans, Lynette. *Extreme Sports* (Shockwave: Social Studies). New York, NY: Scholastic, 2009.

Neelman, Sol. *Weird Sports*. Heidelberg, Germany: Kehrer Verlag, 2011.

**Websites**
**Kidzworld**
*http://www.kidzworld.com/article/2000-quick-facts-on-kite-surfing*
Full of information about kite surfing.

**Underwater Hockey**
*http://www.kidzworld.com/article/14425-wacky-sports-underwater-hockey*
Information about underwater hockey.

**United States Log Rolling Association**
*http://www.uslogrolling.com/html/media.html*
Information about log rolling, with plenty of photographs.

# Index